FIRST NATIONS OF NORTH AMERICA

NORTHWEST COAST INDIANS

LIZ SONNEBORN

HEINEMANN LIBRARY
CHICAGO, ILLINOIS

H **www.heinemannraintree.com**
Visit our website to find out
more information about
Heinemann-Raintree books.

To order:

☎ Phone 888-454-2279
💻 Visit www.heinemannraintree.com
to browse our catalog and order online.

© 2012 Heinemann Library
an imprint of Capstone Global Library, LLC
Chicago, Illinois

Original illustrations © Capstone Global Library, Ltd.
Illustrated by Mapping Specialists, Ltd.
Originated by Capstone Global Library, Ltd.
Printed by China Translation and Printing Company

15 14 13 12 11
10 9 8 7 6 5 4 3 2 1

Library of Congress Cataloging-in-Publication Data
Sonneborn, Liz.
  Northwest Coast Indians / Liz Sonneborn.
    p. cm.—(First nations of North America)
  Includes bibliographical references and index.
  ISBN 978-1-4329-4949-5 (hc)—ISBN 978-1-4329-4960-0
(pb) 1. Indians of North America—Northwest, Pacific—
Juvenile literature. 2. Indians of North America—Northwest,
Pacific—History—Juvenile literature. I. Title.
  E78.N77S63 2012
  979.5004'97—dc22   2010042273

Acknowledgments

The author and publisher are grateful to the following for
permission to reproduce copyright material:

AP Photo: pp. 38, 41 (Darryl Dyck, CP); Corbis: pp. 5 (©
Blaine Harrington III), 10 (© John E Marriott/All Canada
Photos), 18 (© Dan Lamont), 19 (© Seattle Post-Intelligencer
Collection/ Museum of History and Industry), 20 (© Frans
Lanting), 22 (© Canadian Museum of Civilization), 27 (©
Frans Lanting), 28 (© Natalie Fobes), 31 (© Neil Rabinowitz),
37 (© Bettmann); Getty Images: pp. 13 (MPI), 15 (Buyenlarge),
23 (Ted Spiegel/National Geographic), 32 (Hulton Archive),
35 (National Geographic); Library of Congress Prints and
Photographs Division: pp. 12, 14, 21, 24, 26, 29; Nativestock.
com: pp. 16 (© Marilyn Angel Wynn), 30 (© Marilyn Angel
Wynn), 36 (© Marilyn Angel Wynn); Photolibrary: pp. 4 (John
Burke), 8 (George Ostertag/Superstock); Shutterstock: pp. 11
(© James M. House), 25 (© RonGreer.Com).

Cover photograph of a Tlingit totem pole reproduced with
permission from Photolibrary (© AlaskaStock).

We would like to thank Sergei Kan, Ph.D., for his invaluable
help in the preparation of this book.

Every effort has been made to contact copyright holders of
any material reproduced in this book. Any omissions will
be rectified in subsequent printings if notice is given to
the publisher.

All the Internet addresses (URLs) given in this book were valid
at the time of going to press. However, due to the dynamic
nature of the Internet, some addresses may have changed, or
sites may have changed or ceased to exist since publication.
While the author and publisher regret any inconvenience this
may cause readers, no responsibility for any such changes can
be accepted by either the author or the publisher.

Contents

Some words are shown in bold **like this**. You can find out what they mean by looking in the glossary.

Who Were the First People to Live in North America?

This is one version of a story told by the Haida people. The Haida are just one group of American Indians who live in North America. American Indians are the **descendants** of the first humans who arrived on the continent.

Raven was flying high in the sky. He dropped pebbles to the ground below. The pebbles turned into islands called Haida Gwaii.

One day Raven was roaming along the beach on one of the islands. He heard noises coming from a giant clamshell partly buried in the sand. Raven moved closer and saw that it was full of tiny creatures.

Raven was bored and lonely. He decided to coax the creatures out of the shell so he could play with them. The creatures, however, were terrified of Raven.

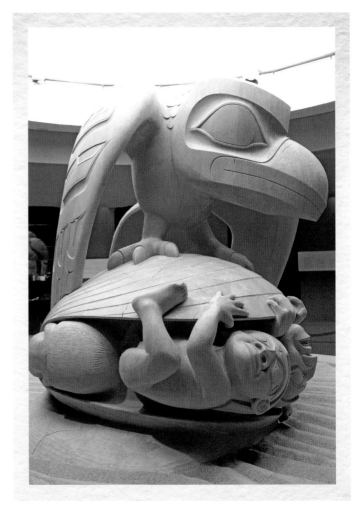

▶ This sculpture, created by Haida artist Bill Reid, shows Raven watching as the first humans crawl out of a giant clamshell.

◄ Descendents of the first people in North America keep the **culture** of their ancestors alive. This girl is dressed to perform a traditional dance of the Tsimshian tribe.

Using his softest voice, Raven tried to calm them. At first, only a few came out to join him. Then more and more emerged from the shell. These creatures were the first people on Earth.

Names for natives

The name "Indian" came from a famous mistake. The Italian explorer Christopher Columbus sailed to North America in the late 1400s. However, he thought he was in India. He called the people he encountered Indians.

The descendants of these people today often prefer to be called American Indians. Others refer to themselves as Native Americans. Some in Canada favor First **Nations**, First Peoples, or Aboriginal Peoples. But many American Indians prefer to be called by the name of their unique group, called a nation or **tribe**—for example, Chinook.

Coming to the Americas

Many scientists now believe that humans first came to North America more than 12,000 years ago. These early people were from the continent of Asia. They were probably hunters chasing after **game**, large animals that can be used for food. Following these animals, they moved into North America by walking across a narrow bridge of land. (Now this land bridge is covered by the waters of the Bering Strait.)

Some scientists believe that humans may have arrived in the Americas even earlier by boat. These people may have come not only from Asia, but also from Australia and Europe.

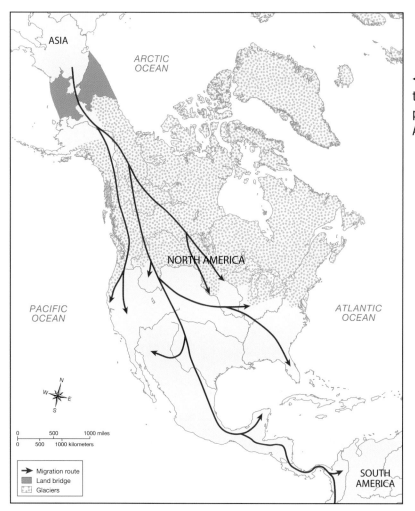

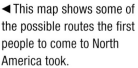

◄ This map shows some of the possible routes the first people to come to North America took.

This map shows the 10 culture areas of North America. Peoples in each culture area tend to have similar ways of life.

Forming tribes

After people arrived in North America, they remained on the move. They eventually spread throughout North and South America. These people came to live in hundreds of separate tribes. Each tribe had its own way of life.

Experts on Indians have grouped these tribes into several **culture areas**. The Indians in each culture area had somewhat similar traditions and beliefs. This book focuses on the native peoples of one culture area—the Northwest Coast. Indians have been living in this region for about 9,000 years.

Who Are the Northwest Coast Indians?

The Northwest Coast **culture area** extends over a long and narrow stretch of land. It includes about 2,000 miles (3,220 kilometers) of the coastline. To the west is the Pacific Ocean. To the east are the high mountains of the Pacific Coast Ranges.

Northwest Coast homelands

The culture area extends into three states in the United States and one **province** in Canada. Far to the area's north is Alaska. The Tlingit live there. Far to the area's south are Washington and Oregon. These states are home to the Chinook, the Makah, the Clatsop, and many smaller groups known as the Coast Salish.

ART AND CULTURE

Rock art

Northwest Coast Indians traditionally created art on the faces of large rocks. These artists used paint or carving instruments to make simple shapes. Some rock art is more than 2,000 years old. In many places in the **Pacific Northwest**, which stretches from northern California to southern Alaska, you can still see this rock art today.

▶ Pictures such as these carved on rock faces by Northwest Coast Indians are called **petroglyphs**.

The middle section of the Northwest Coast culture area is located in the Canadian province of British Columbia. The native peoples of this region include the Heiltsuk, the Tsimshian, and the Kwakwaka'wakw (also called the Kwakiutl).

Several islands in the Pacific Ocean are also part of the Northwest Coast culture area. The Nuu-chah-nulth (also called the Nootka) live on Vancouver Island. The Haida live on the Queen Charlotte Islands and on Prince of Wales Island.

► This map shows where Northwest Coast Indian groups lived before non-Indian contact. Many of their **descendants** live in the same areas today.

A pleasant environment

No matter where they live, Indians of the Northwest Coast are blessed by a comfortable **environment**. Breezes from an ocean current keep the weather relatively warm. Away from the coast, winters are colder. The region is also very rainy, especially in the winter. The Pacific Northwest receives more rain than any area in North America.

The moist air allows big forests of tall trees to flourish. Traditionally, the most important tree for the Northwest Coast Indians was the cedar. These enormous trees provided them with the materials they needed to make houses, clothing, and many other necessities.

Oceans and rivers

Most Northwest Coast Indians lived close to the rocky beaches along the Pacific Coast. Many of their villages were also located near rivers. The Nass and Skeena rivers run through the northern portion of the culture area. The great Columbia River is located in the southern portion.

▲ Lush forests thrive in the warm, rainy weather of the Pacific Northwest.

The nearby ocean and waterways made traveling fairly easy for the Northwest Coast Indians. In **canoes**, they could go from village to village. Travelers might come to a village to trade or just to visit with the people there. They exchanged not just goods, but ideas as well. As a result, even though their customs and languages varied slightly from place to place, the Northwest Coast Indians all shared a similar culture.

▲ Rocky beaches cover the Northwest Coast culture area's coastline, which stretches 2,000 miles (3,220 kilometers).

What Foods Did Early Northwest Coast Indians Eat?

From both the water and the land, Northwest Coast Indians obtained many different types of foods.

Fishing for food

Throughout the region, the most important traditional food source was salmon. This fish spent most of its life in the ocean. But every spring, it swam up rivers to **breed** (have young). During the annual salmon runs, rivers were full of salmon. The fish were so plentiful that fishermen could sometimes pick them out of the water with their hands. More commonly, they used nets or fishing traps called **weirs** to catch as many salmon as they could.

▲ Northwest Coast Indian fishermen built wooden weirs. When fish swam into these traps, fishermen could easily spear them. Northwest Coast peoples still fish this way today.

▲ The Chinook hung dried fish from the ceilings of their houses.

Northwest Coast Indians had a special use for eulachon, also called candlefish. These little fish were very oily. Indians placed wicks inside dried eulachons. When the wick was lit on fire, the fish could serve as a candle.

Halibut and cod were also part of the diet of the Northwest Coast Indians. They made hooks out of bones and wood to catch these fish. They also made fishing rakes. Fishermen scraped these rakes along the ocean floor to scoop up small fish called herring.

Early Northwest Coast Indian women were skilled in preserving fish. They dried fish in the Sun or smoked them over a fire. If preserved properly, the spring catch gave many Northwest Coast Indian groups enough food to last the year.

▲ Makah Indians gather around a whale that has washed ashore. This photo was taken around 1910.

From the ocean

The Pacific Ocean was a rich source of foods other than fish. For much of the year, women could pick up mussels and oysters along the beach. They also gathered clams using a pointed stick to dig them out of the sand.

Hunters ventured into the ocean's waters to stalk sea otters and seals. They killed these animals with clubs and **harpoons**. Harpoons are spears attached to a long rope. Coastal Indians hunted sea animals for both their meat and their fur. The thick furs of sea otters were particularly prized.

Some **tribes**, most notably the Makah and the Nuu-chah-nulth, hunted whales. Whaling was difficult work. But the amount of meat a whale provided was worth it. If a hunter brought home a whale, he could expect to be celebrated as a hero by his entire village.

On land

Early Northwest Coast Indians also hunted land animals. These included deer, bears, and mountain goats. Inland from the coast, they also gathered wild plants for food. A favorite food of the Northwest Coast Indians was berries, including strawberries, raspberries, and blackberries. They used dried berries year-round to flavor many dishes. In what is now Oregon and Washington State, Indians also enjoyed eating the bulb of the **camas**, a type of lily plant. When roasted, camas bulbs taste a little like sweet potatoes.

▲ A Northwest Coast craftsman made these spoons from the horn of an elk.

Where Did Early Northwest Coast Indians Live?

The size and shape of the houses of early Northwest Coast **tribes** varied somewhat. However, most were made of the same material—wooden planks cut from the trunks of cedar trees.

Winter houses

In the **Pacific Northwest**, the winter is the rainy season. As a result, Northwest Coast Indians spent much of the winter indoors. Their winter plank houses were warm and waterproof.

▲ Coastal Indians built their plank houses side-by-side near the ocean. Their doors faced the water.

These large, rectangular houses had no windows. There was, however, a hole in the ceiling. Houses were heated with a central fire, and the hole allowed smoke to escape.

Several related families shared each plank house. Their living areas were separated by mats made from cedar bark. Large cedar chests sometimes also acted as **partitions** (divisions). Families used these chests to store dried foods and valued possessions.

Summer dwellings

When the weather warmed, people left their winter villages. They then traveled to sites that were good for hunting, fishing, and gathering wild plants. Year after year, families went to the same sites. Often they carried with them the planks that formed the walls of their winter houses. Attaching these to wooden frames at their summer sites, they could quickly build temporary houses there.

House paintings

Some Northwest Coast Indian groups painted large animals on the front of their houses. The door often formed the animal's mouth or stomach. These animals were the emblems or the crests of the extended family that occupied the house.

What Did Early Northwest Coast Indians Wear?

Because of the pleasant **climate**, early Northwest Coast Indians often wore little clothing. Men usually went naked, while women wore apron-like skirts. Most of their clothing was woven out of cedar bark. Women soaked the bark in water and beat it with clubs. They then shredded the bark to make a rough yarn.

Hats and robes

Women also used cedar bark to make hats. People wore hats in rainy weather. They were woven so tightly that they were waterproof.

When the weather was cool, Northwest Coast Indians put robes around their shoulders. The warmest robes were made from sea otter furs. Some people also wove blankets from yarn. They made the yarn from the wool of mountain goats or dogs.

▲ Northwest Coast Indians obtained buttons from non-Indian traders. Women used the buttons to make designs on wool blankets.

◄ A Chinook woman with a flattened head holds a baby strapped into a head-flattening device.

The Tlingit are still famous for their Chilkat blankets. These feature complicated designs formed from mountain goat yarn dyed black, yellow, and green.

Jewelry and tattooing

Both men and women liked to wear jewelry made from shells and wood. Many people also decorated their bodies with tattoos. They sometimes used a combination of bear grease and ground-up rocks to redden their skin.

Head flattening

Some early Northwest Coast Indians considered a sloping forehead to be very beautiful. To help their children achieve this look, they strapped the heads of babies in cloth or between two boards to mold their soft skulls. The process was painless, but the head flattening effect was permanent.

What Did Early Northwest Coast Indians Do Everyday?

The daily life of early Northwest Coast Indians depended on their place in society. Everyone had a social rank. In a village, the person with the highest rank was considered the most important. The person with the lowest rank was considered the least important.

Determining rank

Although one's place in society was strongly influenced by one parents' rank, a man or woman could raise his or her status by hard work, generosity, and honorable behavior.

▲ Kwakwaka'wakw leaders come together for a **totem pole** raising **ceremony** in British Columbia.

A few lucky people had a high rank. They were not only the most respected people in their village. They were also the wealthiest.

The least lucky villagers had the lowest rank. They were slaves. Slaves were usually people from other **tribes** who had been taken captive in battle. They had to do the hardest work, such as hauling water and firewood. Sometimes, they were beaten or killed by their owners.

Most people were ranked in the middle of society, between the rich and the enslaved, but they expected to receive support from their wealthier relatives. These high-ranking ones, in turn, could not survive without the cooperation of their lower-ranking relatives.

▶ This young Nuu-chah-nulth woman, photographed in 1910, wears ornaments made of cedar bark in her hair.

A DAY IN THE LIFE OF AN EARLY NORTHWEST COAST INDIAN GIRL

Traditionally, Northwest Coast Indian children were taught early on about the roles they would take on as adults. On a typical day, a girl, for instance, would learn about collecting berries and weaving cedar bark mats by watching and helping her mother. **Elders** (older people) would also teach her how to behave by telling the tribe's old stories. From them, she would learn how to be a good girl and eventually an admired woman.

Making objects

Middle rank people spent much of the spring and summer obtaining and preserving food. With stores of dried fish and berries to get them through the cooler months, they had plenty of spare time in the winter. They used this time to create objects and clothing used in **ceremonies**, as well as practical items. From wood, they made spoons, bowls, and boxes. From cedar bark, they crafted baskets, mats, robes, and hats.

Playing games

In their leisure time, Northwest Coast Indians also played games. Children in many groups played a version of tag. They also played a game in which players stared at each other with a mean expression. The loser was the first player to laugh.

▲ Early Northwest Coast Indians created beautiful wooden boxes carved with animals and spirits. This is a tradition they carry on today.

◄ Haida craftsmen made sculptures out of a black stone called **argillite**, an art form continued to this day.

Adults particularly enjoyed betting games. One involved a stack of carved and painted sticks. Players would separate them into two piles and bet on which pile held the one stick with a special marking.

Teaching children

Children generally learned to do adult work by observing their parents. High-ranking children, however, often received more formal schooling. They were taught special songs, prayers, and stories. These could only be shared with family members and were thought to be very valuable.

Elders also taught children how to behave by telling them stories. Many featured a character named Raven (see pages 4 and 5). Raven was lazy and scheming. Children laughed at and learned from Raven's many mistakes and failures.

Who Were Early Northwest Coast Indian Leaders?

Among early Northwest Coast Indians, leaders were usually men from the most important family in their village. A leader had to be very wealthy. He was expected to share food and other goods with his people.

Leaders generally had a lot of power. They supervised all the shared property of the village. They told their people when to begin the yearly salmon catch. They decided when everyone would leave their winter villages for their summer hunting and gathering sites.

Totem poles

Leaders and their families also had special knowledge. They knew and performed songs that no one else in the village was allowed to sing. Leaders were the only ones who got to use certain high-ranking names and wear certain precious pieces of ceremonial clothing.

▶ **Totem poles** often feature carvings of animals such as bears and ravens.

To remind others of their high rank, leaders and other wealthy people put up totem poles. These were cedar logs painted and carved with their special symbols. Usually leaders hired the best woodworkers they could find to make their totem poles. The tall poles were placed upright in the ground outside of leaders' houses. They were meant to be impressive. They announced that the family who lived in the house deserved respect. The Northwest Coast Indians of today carry on this tradition.

BIOGRAPHY

Honoring Chief Seattle

Seattle is the largest city in Washington State. It was named after the Coast Salish leader known to non-Indians as Chief Seattle. In early 1850s Chief Seattle welcomed non-Indians into his people's lands.

▶ Chief Seattle is remembered today as a great speaker. This statue is in the city of Seattle, Washington.

Potlatches

Leaders also impressed people by hosting **potlatches**. At these gatherings, the host and his family held dances and offered their guests a great feast. The host was also supposed to hand out gifts. To poorer members of the village, the gifts might be food or clothing. But to more important people, they gave more valuable presents. For instance, these guests might expect a sea otter robe or a goat wool blanket. Sometimes even slaves were potlatch gifts.

Potlatches were used to celebrate special events. For instance, a host might hold one to mark a wedding, a funeral, and the naming of a newborn baby. But these get-togethers had another purpose.

▲ A favorite potlatch gift was a portion of a copper. Coppers were shield-like objects made by Northwest Coast craftsmen from natural copper that they found.

They were also a way for leaders and other important people to earn the goodwill of their village. By hosting a potlatch, a leader showed he was a generous person. Poorer villagers were less likely to challenge a leader's authority if they believed he was willing to share his wealth.

With so much at stake, important families competed to throw the most expensive potlatch. In some Northwest Coast societies, a host might set a pile of goods on fire. This was meant to show his guests that he had so much wealth, he could destroy costly possessions without a care.

Some Northwest Coast Indians continue to hold potlatches even though the gifts they give away today are different from the past.

▲ Hosts wanted to impress their potlatch guests by offering them the best gifts they could afford.

What Did Early Northwest Coast Indians Believe?

The early Northwest Coast Indians believed that spirit beings controlled their world. To keep the world in balance, they had to pay proper respect to these spirits. They did so by performing special **ceremonies**.

The First Salmon Ceremony

One of the most important was the First Salmon Ceremony. It was held when a group of fishermen caught the first salmon of the spring fishing season. They cooked and shared the fish's meat. They then returned its bones to the water. If they did not perform the **ritual** properly, the fishermen believed the salmon would not come back to the river the next year.

▲ Through the First Salmon Ceremony (performed here by Tulalip Indians), Northwest Coast Indians show their respect for the salmon, traditionally their most important source of food.

Spiritual leaders

People also sought power from spirit beings through praying and having visions. Especially powerful people were considered spiritual leaders. They were thought to be able to cure the sick. Northwest Coast Indians, however, were a little scared of spiritual leaders. They believed spiritual leaders could use their power to hurt people as well as heal them.

Winter ceremonies

During the winter, the rain and cold forced the Northwest Coast Indians indoors. If they had enough preserved fish and other dried foods, they did not have to worry about getting food. With less work to do, they could devote the unpleasant winter months to preparing for and performing ceremonies.

▲ Northwest Coast Indians spent most of the winter performing ceremonies. They continue to perform these ceremonies today. These two Tlingit men dance during a **potlatch** held in Haines, Alaska.

Ceremonies of the Kwakwaka'wakw

Winter ceremonies were especially elaborate among northern groups such as the Kwakwaka'wakw. Kwakwaka'wakw craftspeople created amazing ceremonial clothing. They are still well known today for their giant masks. The masks were carved from cedar and painted with black, white, and red dyes.

The winter ceremonies were performed by special societies. The most important society was the Hamatsa. Members celebrated a spirit called the Cannibal-at-the-North-End-of-the-World. During one dance, new members of the Hamatsa ran into the audience and began biting (or pretending to bite) people on the arm.

Dancers also used props to make the ceremonies dramatic. For instance, they made puppets of ghosts appear to dance by pulling strings on their arms and legs.

How mosquitoes were created

Northwest Coast Indians told stories to explain their world. This Tlingit tale explained how they believed mosquitoes came to be.

A great giant once lived on Earth. He liked to eat people and drink their blood. One man decided to kill the giant. He stabbed the giant in his heart, which was located in his left heel. As the giant lay dying, he cried that he would never stop eating humans. The man cut up the giant's body and set fire to the parts. When he scattered the ashes in the sky, they turned into mosquitoes. True to the giant's word, these insects still bite people and suck their blood.

▲ Some ceremonial masks were fitted with strings. When a dancer pulled them, pieces of the mask flew open to reveal another mask underneath.

31

When Did Northwest Coast Indians Meet Non-Indians?

In the 1700s, non-Indians began arriving in the Northwest Coast area. The first to meet the Indians there were the Russians and the Spaniards. The Spanish were led by Juan José Pérez Hernández, they encountered the Haida and the Nuu-chah-nulth in 1774.

Four years later, Englishmen led by explorer James Cook again visited the Nuu-chah-nulth. The two groups soon began trading with each other. The Nuu-chah-nulth offered the English animal skins. In return, the English gave the Nuu-chah-nulth metal goods, such as knives and nails.

▲ The Nuu-chah-nulth village at Friendly Cove was visited by English traders in the late 1700s.

The fur trade

Other non-Indians came to the **Pacific Northwest** to trade. They were from Russia and the eastern United States.

Non-Indians were especially interested in trading for sea otter furs. These furs were popular in China. Traders could make great fortunes by shipping the furs to China and selling them there.

The Northwest Coast Indians were eager to trade with these outsiders. They wanted the metal goods they offered. They had not seen such goods before contact with non-Indians, but they immediately saw how useful they could be. For instance, guns made hunting easier and axes made house-building quicker.

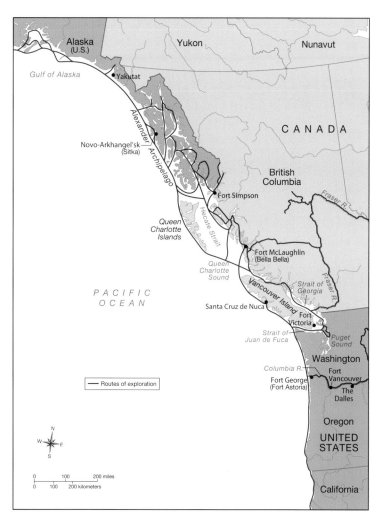

▲ This map shows the routes non-Indian traders and explorers took to the Pacific Northwest in the 1700s and early 1800s

LANGUAGE

Chinook Jargon

Indian and non-Indian traders in the Pacific Northwest spoke different languages. To help them communicate, they developed a special trading language. It was called Chinook Jargon. Chinook Jargon included words from Spanish, Russian, English, and several Indian languages. Easy to learn, it allowed traders of all backgrounds to make deals with each other.

How Did Life Change for Northwest Coast Indians?

By the mid-1800s, non-Indians were coming to the **Pacific Northwest** not just to trade. They were coming there to live. Many were farmers, attracted by the rich lands in the area, others were prospectors looking for gold.

Losing land

As more of their citizens moved there, the governments of the United States and Canada claimed to own the Indians' homelands. In 1846 these two countries signed a **treaty**. It said Northwest Coast Indian lands in present-day Washington state and Oregon belonged to the United States. Their lands in present-day British Columbia belonged to Canada. (The portion of the Northwest Coast **culture area** in what is now Alaska became part of the United States in 1867.)

Soon, Americans and Canadians took over the homelands of the Northwest Coast Indians. Some Indian groups were left landless. Others were confined to small areas. In the United States, these areas were called **reservations**. In Canada, they were called **reserves**.

Dying from disease

In addition to losing their land, many Northwest Coast Indians also lost their lives. Non-Indians carried germs for smallpox, measles, and other diseases. Indian peoples had never been exposed to these diseases, so their bodies had no natural defenses against them. These diseases killed many Northwest Coast Indians.

Many **elders** died of disease. They were therefore not able to pass along their knowledge of Indian customs and languages to younger people. In this way, Northwest Coast Indians lost much of their old way of life.

▲ These women, photographed in 1960, are preparing salmon steaks to be eaten at a **potlatch** feast.

▲ In the Pacific Northwest, many Indian children attended government boarding schools. There, they were taught how to speak English and dress and act like non-Indians. These two photos show how the children looked before and after going to a government boarding school.

A changing culture

Non-Indians also forced many Indians to abandon their **tribal** ways. Some people who tried to do this were **missionaries**. These people wanted Indians to give up their religion and become Christians. Suspicious of Indian customs, the Canadian government also outlawed potlatches. More and more, it became difficult for Northwest Coast **tribes** to perform **ceremonies** that united them as a people. In more remote communities, like southeastern Alaska, traditional ceremonies continued.

Indians were also unable to obtain food in the ways they had in the past. As non-Indians took over many of their lands, Indians could no longer go to many of their traditional hunting and fishing sites. Just to survive, many had to start working for non-Indians for low pay.

Defying the potlatch ban

In 1884 the Canadian government outlawed the potlatch. One Kwakwaka'wakw leader explained why he refused to obey this law:

> We will dance when our laws command us to dance, we will feast when our hearts desire to feast. Do we ask the white man, "Do as the Indian does"? No we do not. Why then do you ask us, "Do as the white man does"?
>
> It is a strict law that bids us dance. . . . It is a good law. Let the white man observe his law, we shall observe ours.

▲ By the late 1800s, most Northwest Coast Indians could no longer make their living off the land. Instead, they had to accept low-paying wage work, like these Indian men in Oregon, who are shown training to become blacksmiths.

What Is Life Like Today for Northwest Coast Indians?

Northwest Coast Indians still live in the United States and Canada. In many ways, their lives are like those of their non-Indian neighbors. But many Indians continue to have a strong connection to their land and to their **tribal** relatives. Together, they work to improve their communities and better the lives of their people.

Fighting for their rights

In the later 1900s, coastal **tribes** in Washington State fought for access to their traditional fishing sites. As a result, a large number of Northwest Coast Indians still make their living by fishing.

▲ In the late 1960s, Indians of Washington state held protests to help them regain their fishing rights.

Many tribes have also worked to get official recognition, which would make them eligible for health care and other benefits, from the U.S. government. Others have battled in court to regain control of their traditional lands.

In the United States and Canada, Indian groups have fought for religious freedom. They now perform **ceremonies** that were once discouraged or outlawed. For instance, the Kwakwaka'wakw and other northern groups continue to hold **potlatches** today.

Preserving Indian cultures

Some Northwest Coast Indians tribes have preserved their **culture** by creating museums. One is the Haida Gwaii

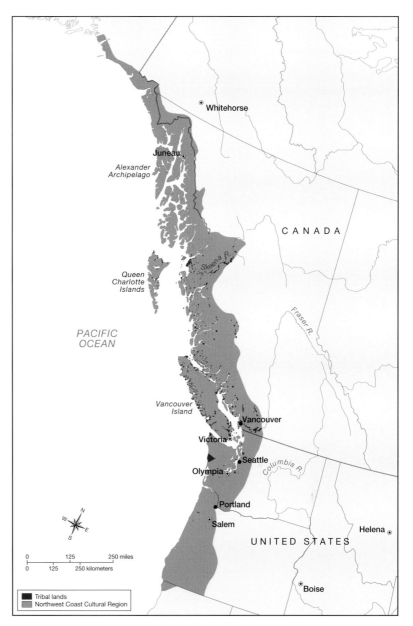

▲ This map shows **reservations** and **reserves** where some Northwest Coast Indians live today.

Museum in British Columbia. It features exhibits of **totem poles** and other objects made long ago by Haida craftspeople. Museums around the world also display traditional Northwest Coast Indian masks and carvings. They are now recognized as works of art.

Northwest Coast Indian artists

Today, Northwest Coast Indian artists make modern works that draw on their people's artistic traditions. For instance, in his glass sculptures, Tlingit artist Preston Singletary reproduces symbols that have long been used by his people.

Some Northwest Coast artists make their living by carving totem poles. In 2004 carvers from the Lummi tribe created two totem poles called *Liberty* and *Freedom*. These poles honored the victims of the terrorist attack on the Pentagon in Washington, D.C., on September 11, 2001.

BIOGRAPHY

Bill Reid

As a young man, Bill Reid (1920-1998) studied the work of the great Haida carver Charles Edenshaw. Edenshaw, a distant relative of Reid's, inspired him to become a sculptor. Throughout his career, Reid helped to revive knowledge of Haida carving techniques. He also used images and symbols found in traditional Haida artwork. (See page 4 for an example of his artwork.)

Tribal Journeys

The Makah continue to **canoe** in the Pacific Ocean. Along with many other Northwest Coast Indians, they participate in Tribal Journeys. During this annual event, people enjoy traditional dancing and singing, while teams **navigate** dozens of traditional canoes through the ocean. By canoeing through the Pacific's choppy waters, young Northwest Coast Indians celebrate their tribal history and culture.

▲ Thousands of Northwest Coast Indians participate in Tribal Journeys each year.

Timeline

about 7,000 BCE	Humans arrive in the Northwest Coast **culture area**.
about 4,000 BCE	People in the **Pacific Northwest** learn how to preserve fish.
1741 CE	Russian explorers and fur traders begin arriving in Alaska via the Aleutian Islands.
1774	A Spanish crew led by Juan José Pérez Hernández encounters the Haida and the Nuu-chah-nulth.
1778	English captain James Cook trades with the Nuu-chah-nulth at Nootka Sound.
1792	U.S. fur trader Robert Gray sails the Columbia River.
1803	Nuu-chah-nulth warriors led by Maquinna attack and kill most of the U.S. crew of a ship called the *Boston*.
1805	U.S. explorers Meriwether Lewis and William Clark spend the winter among the Chinook and the Clatsop.
1846	The northwestern boundary between the United States and what is now Canada is established.
1850s	The United States negotiates a series of **treaties** to gain control of Indian land in Washington state and Oregon.
1862-3	An outbreak of smallpox kills at least 20,000 Northwest Coast Indians.
1867	The United States purchases Alaska from Russia.
1876	Canada defines its policies toward American Indians in the Canadian Indian Act.
1882	The U.S. Navy destroys the Tlingit village of Angoon.

1884   The Canadian government outlaws the **potlatch ceremony**.

1886   Anthropologist Franz Boas begins studying the **culture** of the Kwakwaka'wakw.

1922   Eighty Kwakwaka'wakw are arrested for holding a potlatch.

1958   Queen Elizabeth II of England commissions a **totem pole** from Kwakwaka'wakw carver Mungo Martin as part of British Columbia's centennial (100-year) celebration.

1970   The long-buried ancient Makah village of Ozette is uncovered.

1971   Alaska Native Claims Settlement Act is signed into law.

1974   A court delivers the "Boldt decision", which grants **tribes** in western Washington State 50 percent of the annual salmon harvest.

1974   Tribes in Washington State establish the Northwest Indian Fisheries Commission.

1989   Representatives of 17 Northwest Coast tribes **navigate** dugout **canoes** during the "Paddle to Seattle" celebration.

1999   The Makah hold their first whale hunt since the 1920s.

2004   A new Canadian $20 bill features the artwork of Haida sculptor Bill Reid.

2008   The Haida celebrate the grand opening of the Haida Heritage Center.

2009   Queen Charlotte Islands officially renamed Haida Gwaii (home of the Haida people)

Glossary

argillite black stone the Haida used to make sculptures

breed to produce a certain kind of animal or plant by human care

camas plant in the lily family with an edible bulb

canoe light, narrow boat

ceremony religious event or observance

climate normal weather conditions in a particular area

culture shared ways of life and beliefs of a group of people

culture area region of North America in which Indians traditionally had a similar way of life

descendant offspring of an earlier group

elder older person

environment natural surroundings

game wild animals hunted for food

harpoon spear attached to a long rope

missionary person who tries to persuade others to adopt his or her religion

nation unified group of native people in North America

navigate to direct a boat on a specific coast

Pacific Northwest area of land along the Pacific Coast of North America that stretches from northern California to southern Alaska

partition structure that separates one part of a room from the rest of it

petroglyph design carved into a rock face

potlatch feast held by some American Indian tribes, during which the host offers gifts to his or her guests

province area in Canada that is similar to a state in the United States

reservation area of land in the United States put aside for the use of American Indians

reserve area of land put aside for the use of native peoples of Canada by the government

ritual formal acts or series of acts performed according to a set of rules, often having to do with religion

totem pole pole carved and painted with animals and spirit beings

treaty agreement, especially one between two or more countries

tribal relating to a tribe

tribe group of American Indians who share a culture

weir fence set into water that is used as a trap to catch fish

Find Out More

Books

Belarde-Lewis, Miranda. *Meet Lydia: A Native Girl from Southeast Alaska*. Tulsa: Smithsonian National Museum of the American Indian, in association with Council Oak Books, 2004.

De Capua, Sarah. *The Tlingit*. New York: Marshall Cavendish, 2010.

King, David C. *The Haida*. New York: Marshall Cavendish Benchmark, 2007.

Peterson, Judy Monroe. *The Northwest Indians: Daily Life in the 1700s*. Mankato, Minn.: Capstone, 2006.

Websites

American Indians of the Pacific Northwest Collection
http://content.lib.washington.edu/aipnw
This site offers a searchable database with more than 2,000 photographs relating to the cultures of Northwest Coast and Plateau Indians.

Canadian Museum of Civilization
www.civilization.ca/cmc/exhibitions/aborig/grand/grandeng.shtml
This website features photographs from the Candaian Museum of Civilization's exhibit of six traditional Northwest Coast Indian houses.

Makah Tribe's Website on Whaling
www.makah.com/whaling.html
The official website of the Makah tribe explains its tradition of whale hunting and the attempts to revive whale hunting in modern Makah culture.

Northwest Coast Indian History and Culture
www.anchoragemuseum.org/galleries/alaska_gallery/NW_indian.aspx
The Anchorage Museum in Alaska offers an online exhibition of objects in its collection made by Tlingit, Haida, and Tsimshian artists.

Places to visit

Alaska Native Heritage Center Museum
Anchorage, AK
http://alaskanative.genclik.ca

The Burke Museum of Natural History and Culture
University of Washington
Seattle, WA
www.washington.edu/burkemuseum

Haida Heritage Centre
Skidgate, Haida Gwaii
British Columbia, Canada
www.haidaheritagecentre.com

National Museum of the American Indian
Fourth Street and Independence Avenue, SW
Washington, D.C.
www.nmai.si.edu

Further research

What parts of the Northwest Coast lifestyle did you find the most interesting? How does life for native peoples in the Northwest Coast compare to the way native peoples live today in other regions? How did the peoples who first lived in your area contribute to life today? To learn more about the Northwest Coast or other culture areas, visit one of the suggested places on these pages or head to your local library for more information.

Index